Christmas 09

To Fa

C000246424

They
tickle you - I'll look
forward to hearing
some from the horses
month !!

Xx Bea xx.

SERVICE SLANG

SERVICE SLANG

a first selection

collected and edited by
FLYING-OFFICER J. L. HUNT
and
LIEUT. A. G. PRINGLE, R.A.

with a foreword by
AIR-MARSHALL SIR T. L. LEIGH-MALLORY
K.C.B., D.S.O.
A.O.C. in Chief, Fighter Command

illustrated by
FLYING-OFFICER C. MORGAN

faber and faber

First published in 1943
by Faber and Faber Limited
This edition first published in 2008
by Faber and Faber Limited
3 Queen Square London WCIN 3AU

Printed in England by Mackays of Chatham, plc

A CIP record for this book
is available from the British Library

ISBN 978-0-571-24014-2

2 4 6 8 10 9 7 5 3 1

FOREWORD

by Air-Marshal Sir T. L. Leigh-Mallory
K.C.B., D.S.O.

No doubt the hair of the purists will turn grey when they read these pages. If so, I would explain that Flying-Officer Hunt has tried to record the full-blooded language of fighting men—men who won the Battle of Britain, are winning many other battles and who will eventually restore peace to the world. I am proud to command men who give every ounce they have in the fight, and when peace is won this book may remind them of many sad and many happy times which helped them to coin new words or apply new meanings to old ones. It is a book of slang, yet I recommend it to you because it records the language of men of the three services of many countries who, to borrow a phrase from the book, are 'flat out' to win.

T. LEIGH-MALLORY
Air-Marshal

21 *April* 1943

WARNING

The reader should approach *Service Slang* in the right frame of mind. Briefly, he should be grateful for what he can get. He should bear in mind that this is an attempt to plot something that is continuously changing. If he is one of those readers who expect to find the origin of each phrase pinpointed, he must revise his ideas. There can be few books for which so little research was possible and on which so little has been wasted.

In one sense, no book of slang which can be printed can be entirely representative. The habitual indecency of the Anglo-Saxon male in retirement must be known to be believed. It is often associated with the kindliest feelings and is probably most due to a refusal to take anything outside the job seriously, for which there is much to be said in wartime.

Not every entry in our alphabet is slang in the strict sense of the word. At the same time, the reader should remember that this is a book of service slang, not of service jargon and abbreviation. Nor can we claim that all the expressions originated in one or other of the services. It is clear, especially with the Cockney bits and pieces, that many of them derive from civil life.

The real difficulty in making a selection of this kind is that to do justice to all the services and their various branches nothing short of a committee of representatives would be needed. And a further snag is the fact that R.A.F. fighting slang (conceived in a new medium and born of new achievements) is not only contemporary and interesting in a way that neither Army nor Naval slang can be, but also, for reasons that are equally obvious, far more accessible in this country than, say, the latest coinings of our armies in the Middle East. We might have

7

done better, therefore, to stick to R.A.F. slang (which is often indebted to Naval slang), but we preferred to do our best all round, without, however, delving too far into traditions, which are already far better expounded elsewhere than we could hope to explain them here.

What we have tried to give is something to represent the day-to-day life and characteristic imagination of the serviceman through his speech, which would be of interest to his relatives and friends, and of assistance to any who may be about to join him.

CONTENTS

9

Ack-ack. Short for 'anti-aircraft'. ('Ac' was used in the services' phonetic alphabet for sending the letter 'A'. It often stands for 'assistant'; an Assistant Instructor in Gunnery, written A.I.G., is always called an Ac I.G., and the Gun Position Officer's Assistant is the G.P.O. Ac.)

The Admiral. The Officer in charge of the R.A.F. Air-Sea Rescue boats.

Ados. Assistant Director of Ordnance Services—recently banished from the hierarchy of DOS, and replaced by D.D.O.S. (Deputy Director, etc.).

Adrift. Overdue from leave or late pass.

Afters. The pudding or cheese. ('What's for afters?')

Airmaids. Crew of the Air-Sea Rescue boats.

Alert. Officer or N.C.O. approaching!

All clear. Games may continue.

All right? In the Army, instruction, lectures, and verbal orders are heavily punctuated by this phrase, meaning 'Is that clear?' (itself a favourite).

All right for YOU. An ironical greeting and reference to another's job in comparison with your own. Used, for instance, when troops travelling in a truck pass others on foot.

Any questions? This, the correct conclusion to an operation order, is also the ultimate 'All right?' of an Army lecture. But as it is usually time for a break at this point, the odd man who asks a question is likely to make himself unpopular.

Ammo. Ammunition.

And like it! A Naval expression anticipating a grouse and added to any instruction for an awkward or unwanted job.

Andrew Miller. The Navy.

Angels. The R.A.F. use this symbolic word to give heights when flying and it is part of the code employed in the Battle of Britain. '20 M.E.s at Angels one owe' means '20 Messerschmitts at 10,000 ft.'

11

ANNIE

Annie. The old Anson aircraft, now used as a trainer.

Are you happy in your work? A purely facetious question addressed to anyone who has been saddled with some embarrassing task.

An Arrival. The safe landing of aircraft.

Arthur. Arsine gas.

Ashcan. Wasted time.

Asparagus bed. A form of anti-tank obstacle, designed to slow up the A.F.V. while it comes under fire.

At. Member of the Auxiliary Territorial Service.

Adjutant's At. A blonde member of the above.

Atterize. To staff with A.T.S., or a proportion of A.T.S., e.g. to man static gun sites with mixed batteries.

Attery. Living quarters occupied by the A.T.S.

Bad types. Chaps who are always eager to organize and go out to parties.

Baffle. A Royal Corps of Signals expression for elaborate Security measures.

Bag. Parachute.

Bags of brace. Drill bombardier's exhortation to his squad.

Bags of mystery. Sausages, of course.

Balbo. A large formation of aircraft, so called after the famous flight of the Italian air armada from Italy to South America, led by the late Marshal of that name.

Bale out. Abandon the plane in mid-air by parachute.

Banana boat. An invasion barge.

Bandstand. R.A.F. nickname for the cruet in the Officers' Mess. In Ack-Ack, the Command Post of a gun position.

Bang on. Bomber slang for 'O.K.' or 'Everything's all right'.

Bang water. Canadian term for petrol, also called FIRE WATER.

Barkers. An old Army name for sausages, which is especially common overseas.

Bashers. Instructors in physical training.

Battle wagon. A sailor's name for a battleship. A soldier's name for an expensive motor-car, like the Brigadier's.

Batty. Batman or batwoman.

The Beach. The land as opposed to the sea.

A Beat-up. Ground strafing; also, a very lively visit to the local, or a good party in Mess.

Beaverette. A light armoured car.

Bed down. To retire [or the act of retiring] for sleep. One must agree that this is a real contribution to the language of human affairs and one which deserves a currency beyond the limits of its derivation.—In the morning bedding is rolled 'up' when kits are laid out for inspection; and, as country people know, horses are 'bedded down' for the night.

Beef. An alternative term to the famous BIND [q.v.], but only applicable to the crime itself, of boring one's colleagues by retailing shop-news and stale information.

Beehive. Close formation of bombers with fighter escort.

Beer-beer. Nothing to do with the wine of the country, but the old services' alphabetic abbreviation of Balloon Barrage.

Beer lever. Part of the controls of an aircraft; the 'joystick'.

Belly landing. Landing with the undercarriage up, when it is impossible to get the wheels of the plane down.

Best blue. An airman's walking-out suit and the better of the two issued to him. The term is used officially, in the same sense as 'best battledress' in the Army, when men are detailed for special parades.

Blues. A soldier's dark blue walking-out dress embellished with the colours of his Arm or Regiment. He buys a set of blues out of his own pocket if he wants one.

Big eats. A good spread; an exceptionally good day at the cookhouse.

Billjims. Nickname for Australian soldiers and airmen.

13

Bin. Living quarters in which the rooms are very small.

Bind. This must be the most used of all Air Force slang expressions. It may describe a person who bores with out-of-date news or who is always in the know [see also RIGID BIND]. It is also used for the act of boring, whence comes BINDER, one who binds, and by extension both noun and verb may refer to such antisocial behaviour as moaning (which is distinct from grousing, the serviceman's privilege) or working in one's spare time.

Binding rigid. The act of continually retailing stale information or endeavouring to create an impression by SHOOTING THE LINE.

Bint. The service name for one's girl friend. Thus, a LUSH BINT.

Biscuits. The three miniature mattresses issued to servicemen for bedding. This is an old joke since a recruit invariably thinks of food and believes that his leg is being pulled when he is told that he will sleep on biscuits.

A Black. A black mark for doing something badly.

Black bourse. A comprehensive term used in connection with rationing where the general public is concerned. In the service it covers the out-of-hours sale of cigarettes, for example.

Black-out. Temporary loss of consciousness before pulling out of a power dive. BLACK-OUT, to experience this.

Bleat. Complaint or grouse.

Blister. A protuberance above or below the fuselage of a plane enclosing a gun position.

A Blitz. This well-worn expression is converted by servicemen for the spring clean which takes place when important officials are expected. There is also a verb BLITZ, which means to descend upon your juniors in wrath.

Blitz buggies. A nice piece of slang which unmistakably suggests that ambulances are to be used during to-night's exercises, but which may also refer to any *fast* transport vehicles.

Blitz-ridden. Damaged beyond repair.

Bloke. A chap or WALLAH of any description. Barely distinguishable in use from the latter, though WALLAH possibly suggests something faintly pontifical about a bloke. A GOOD BLOKE is a sound man. In Naval slang, THE BLOKE is the Commanding Officer.

Blonde job. A fair-haired member of the W.A.A.F.

Blood wagon. Ambulance.

The Blower. Signals use this as their name for the telephone. Other sections have their pet names which will be found in the following pages.

Blue-caps. Service Police.

Blue job. Policeman; or the Navy.

Blue-light. A Warrant gunner.

Bobbing. This is the act of endeavouring to 'creep' or curry favour with one's N.C.O. or Officer [taken, we presume, from the old-fashioned curtsey].

Body Snatchers

Body snatcher. Man detailed for a first-aid party. If on duty during an air raid, he is known as a 'body snatcher in a flap'.

A Bogus. A person who is caught out in a pretence or sham.

Bomb. Familiar mode of address to a Bombardier.

15

Bonce. A name for one's head.

Bondhook. Overseas slang for one's rifle, and common throughout the Regular Army.

Bonza. The Australian troops' word for O.K.

Booping. Crying or making a lot of fuss about a trivial matter.

Borrow. To acquire by fair means or foul.

A Bottle. A dressing-down. [The Navy.]

Bottled sunshine. Scottish service name for beer.

Bounce. To be returned by the Bank [of a dud cheque]. 'And, Gentlemen, whatever you do, never, *never* sign a cheque that is going to bounce.'

Bowler hat. The symbol of a return to civil life, e.g. of an Officer found unsuitable. Hence BOWLER-HATTED.

Bows down. Naval way of telling someone, usually a bore, to 'dry up'.

Bow waves. A word used by the Canadians to describe sailors who are new to the sea.

Box clever. To avoid being posted or to escape unwanted fatigues one must use a little initiative. 'Boxing clever' means saving one's legs by using one's head. [R.A.F.]

Brassed off. Mildly BROWNED OFF [q.v.], or in the very first stages of being browned off; not yet quite CHEESED OFF. The verb BRASS OFF means to tell off severely. In other words, one may feel brassed off after having been brassed off. [Probably derived from the duty of polishing brasses.]

Brass-hat. Still used for any Army Officer wearing a red cap band—Colonel or above, or Staff Officer.

Brassy. Sailor slang for a friend, a pal. [See PARTING BRASS-RAGS.]

Break. R.A.F. word for short leave periods; week-ends or two-day privilege 'breaks' come under this heading. In the Army it means what it meant at school—'the morning break'—when under favourable conditions the N.A.A.F.I. opens or the mobile canteen comes round; or it can be used for any short rest period in the middle of a job, like the famous 'five minutes' break for a smoke'.

Break off. To end a combat, or [in the ranks] to end a conversation when N.C.O.s or Officers are observed; in Army terminology, to cease work and start a break.

Bricks. The unofficial title of the Air Ministry Works and Buildings Department. Although sometimes called 'the many who do so little for the few', this department performs essential work in building and maintaining our aerodromes and station buildings.

Brig. The cells. [Naval equivalent of JANKERS.]

Brock's benefit. Bomber slang for a particularly large display of enemy searchlights, flares, and ack-ack fire.

Brolly. A pilot's name for his parachute.

Brolly hop. A jump from an aircraft by parachute.

Browned off. Up to the autumn of 1942, the most important of all service slang expressions; and father and mother of a whole series of similar expressions. Possibly its inventor saw himself as a piece of meat that had too long been cooking. It is also suggested that the phrase originates in that notable lobstertan which all soldiers, sailors, and airmen seem to acquire. But it is a state of mind that is described, and, to investigate this, the mod-

Browned Off

est soul of the serviceman must be laid bare. This condition, then, has a positive as well as a negative aspect. A man who has been doing some apparently unpleasant or monotonous job for what seems to be a long time may say quite cheerfully that he is 'browned off *to* it', and such a man is no longer the creature of naïve enthusiasm and violent dislike so far as his attitude to that job is concerned. On the other hand, and much more commonly, people say simply that they are browned off, or browned off *with* something. Depressed, bored, fed up—all the words we used to know denote too much egotism and self-pity to explain what is meant. It is a kind of indifference, a state in which personal feelings and interests appear to have been suspended while the disciplined cog goes through the normal motions; the cause may be stoppage of pay or leave or return from leave, and it is just as often the fact of having been pushed from place to place or taken off one unfinished job after another as it is the monotony of routine. Another use of the phrase which should be noted is the transitive verb. A Sergeant-Major, for instance, has it in his power to 'brown off' a junior N.C.O. or man who makes a nuisance of himself.

In conclusion, the use of this expression should never be taken too seriously, since it has long been the approved custom to answer any inquiry as to one's health in these terms.

Brown food. Beer.

Brown job. The Army [R.A.F. name].

Brylcreem boys. The R.A.F. [Army name].

Bubble-dancing. Pot-washing in the cookhouse, whether as a duty or a fatigue.

A Bucket. A formation of aircraft shaped like a bucket.

Buckshee. The good old Army slang for 'free' or 'gratis', adapted from the Indian beggar's appeal for alms, 'Baksheesh'.

A Bull. To hit the nail on the head in an argument is to register a bull, as in the game of darts or on the rifle range.

Bullets. Peas.

* * *. A coarse expression of transatlantic origin, associated in American college life with stag parties and cock-and-bull stories, and widely used between men in the services. By this they mean anything that they regard as eyewash, rubbish, and pure bluff—external show unsupported, as they see it, by necessity, achievement, or knowledge—whether perpetrated by the individual for his own advancement or enforced by higher authority. On the other hand, an old soldier may sometimes say defensively that 'a bit of * * * is good for the troops'—because a man newly called up from civil life may not appreciate his standards of smartness, and mistake them for * * *.

Bumph. The schoolboy's rude word for toilet paper has a disproportionate importance in wartime. All tedious instructions on paper, all apparently useless documents, all official correspondence considered only fit for the wastepaper basket is known as 'bumph'. The word is also used for leaflets dropped from the air: hence the portmanteau 'bumphleteers' for those engaged in dropping them. 'Bumph from above' descends from higher formations and not from the air.

Bumping bag. Air cushion [American Air Force].

Bumps. The touching down of the aircraft during landing due to uneven ground or bad handling; or a condition of the air giving rise to bumpy flying when the weather is unfavourable.

Bung hole. An Army name for bread.

Bunting tosser. Sailor's name for a signaller.

Burgoo. Army for porridge.

Bus driver. The pilot of a bomber, so called because he is usually on a well-beaten route and does not have to chase an enemy over an unprepared course.

Bust. To reduce to the ranks or to a lower rank; to deprive an N.C.O. of his stripes. Hence BUSTED.

Butter. The use of honeyed words in an endeavour to get time off, to get excused fatigues, and suchlike.

Buttoned up. To have the job or situation well in hand, and to feel quite competent, is to have it 'buttoned up'. This is what bomber pilots and their crews say after the preliminary run-in over targets, before the load is released. Similarly, WRAPPED UP, which might be used by a class of cadets after a technical lecture.

Button your flap. A terse Naval way of saying 'Be quiet.'

A Buzz. The Naval word for Rumour, adopted by the R.A.F.

The Buzzer. Another name for the telephone, and particularly the modern 'buzz' boxes or house-phone systems.

Cage. A British camp for Axis prisoners of war, as in the North African desert.

Cake hole. The airman's name for his or anyone else's mouth.

Can. (*a*) Guardroom or jail.

(*b*) That which is carried, i.e. the responsibility or the blame.

Carrying the can back. Accepting the blame for your own or another's error. It is customary to state that you are doing this even when it is a well-known fact that you did commit the offence. One rarely hears an admission of guilt in the services, it just isn't done lest too much confession should be interpreted as BOBBING.

Cannucks. Canadian soldiers.

Can't claim halfpenny. A complete alibi which is carefully concocted when one is about to face a charge.

Canteen medals. Beer stains on a man's tunic.

Cape of Good Hope. Cockney for soap has caught on again after a successful run during the last war. (Unfortunately we have space here for only a few of the many articles of rhyming slang.)

Cast-iron. Irrefutable or BULLET-PROOF.

Catch a cold. To get oneself into trouble by being too impetuous.

Cats. Catalina aircraft of Coastal Command.

Cat's eyes. Nickname for the pilots of our night-fighter squadrons who are, as results testify, able to see the enemy in the dark.

Cat's walk. The long plank on bomber aircraft stretching between cockpit and tail.

In the Can

Caught with your trousers down. Caught unprepared or napping.

Caulk. A Naval expression for sleep.

C.B. 'Confined to barracks'. Thus, 'Awarded 7 days' C.B.'

Ceiling. The height at which a plane can fly or is flying; also, the limit to which a man will go when his card-hand is good. It will be noticed that the old equation cieling = sky has been reversed.

The Champagne glass. The Hampden or the Hereford bomber (plan view).

21

Chancer. One who tries it on by TELLING THE TALE; or one who just takes chances. Hence (or from) CHANCING YOUR ARM.

Char. The favourite beverage sometimes known as tea. [From the Hindustani.]

Char-wallah. In India this is a native servant who brings the early morning tea. In Gibraltar, a dining-hall waiter.

Charlie Noble. The galley funnel.

Charmer. Nickname for a girl friend.

Chase. To run after people and see that they do their job.

Chat. Army slang for a louse.

Chatty. Troubled in this way.

Chatterbox. Americanism for machine-gun, now used by pilots and air crews generally. We have to thank the Eagle Squadrons for this and other American phrases.

Cheesecutter. A Cavalryman's sword.

Cheesed off. More than BRASSED OFF; yet not entirely BROWNED OFF.

Chicago piano. A multiple pom-pom gun.

Chief buffer. Chief Boatswain's Mate.

Chiefie. Patronizing term for one's senior N.C.O.

My China. Affectionate way of referring to one's best friend.

Chin food. The conversation of a BINDER.

Chippy. Slang for carpenter, and used in all the services.

Chocker. This is the sailor's way of saying he is fed up or browned off.

Chiefie

22

Chocks away. Get on with the job! i.e. remove the wooden chocks and let the plane get off the ground.

Choky. Detention. [Expressive of confinement and the cell.]

Chow. Slang for food; another word for this is CHUFF.

Chummie. This endearment does not necessarily indicate a mellow intimacy. Two Cockney soldiers who have just met on a vegetable-peeling fatigue may expostulate with 'Listen, chummie' as the discussion grows warm.

Civvy. A recruit who is waiting for his uniform, or a civilian employee.

Civvy Street. One's pre-war occupation; civilian life. In the old days most of us were 'working in Civvy Street', as it is invariably called.

The Clever boys. People who work things out on paper; people with theoretical knowledge.

The really clever boys. People with positively academic knowledge.

The white-bearded boys. People who establish unintelligible principles and prove them, like the ballisticians of Woolwich.

Clew up. To fix one's hammock by the clew system; thus, to join a new ship.

Clinker-knocker. A ship's stoker.

Clippies. Girls who work on buses and trams.

Close hangar doors. Stop talking shop.

Close stick. A stick of bombs dropped to explode in a small area, as opposed to an open stick.

A Clot. One who is unusually slow on the uptake.

The Club. The propeller or airscrew.

Clubs. Naval nickname for the physical training instructor, whose badge is the crossed Indian clubs.

Coat of arms. Worn by Regimental Sergeant-Majors and other Warrant Officers, Class One. If and when a man is promoted to this majestic rank he is said to 'have his coat of arms up'. [Cf. CROWN].

Cob on. To sulk, to take offence, to get angry.

Cold steel. Bayonet.

Comedian. Commandant. Men referred to the 'Camp Comedian' have sometimes spent hours searching for an Entertainments Department instead of going to the right quarter.

Come the old soldier. To bluff like an OLD SOLDIER [q.v.].

Coming and going. [Of a plane.] Fitted with wireless.

The Camp Comedian

Common. Common sense. Thus, 'a bit of common'; and 'Use your common', which is the same as USE YOUR LOAF.

Conchie. The most widely accepted term for a man who objects to taking an active or, to be accurate, a fighting part in the services.

Con course. When a man remusters from one trade to another, for instance if a clerk wishes to become an armourer, he takes a course and this is called a conversion course. 'Con course' more often than not refers to the change-over of armament on aircraft, like the conversion of Blenheim bombers into fighters.

Confetti. American name for machine-gun bullets.

Conner. The B.E.F. gave us this word after living on tinned food for weeks—it is an abbreviation of the manufacturers' name.

24

Conservatory. The enclosed portion of an aircraft; sometimes the cockpit, but more often the converted accommodation as in the Hudson bombers. [So called because of the 'glass' roofing. See other pages for further 'gen' on this subject.]

The Constable. Unwanted person who attaches himself to another; a hanger-on who refuses to take the hint.

Cookery nook. The galley aboard ship, or the cookhouse on shore stations.

The Cooler. The Guardroom or detention barracks.

Copper-knockers. The metalworkers' shop on an aerodrome.

Corduroy brigade. Another Works and Buildings expression [see BRICKS], meaning the actual workmen, plumbers, bricklayers.

Corny. Of small matter and hardly worth mentioning. [Students of swing will think of a 'corny', or hackneyed, trumpet solo.]

Courting a cat. Taking a girl out (according to the Navy).

Crabbing along. Flying near the ground; HEDGE HOPPING.

A Crack. An attempt or try. [See also DART and STAB.]

Crack down. To shoot down [a Hun plane].

Crack down on. To suppress [undisciplined persons or unlawful acts].

Crack down on the deck. To crash on the airfield or on the ground. Equally applicable to a forced landing in the eyes of 'star' pilots.

Crash landing. A landing with the undercarriage up or a forced landing due to some other mechanical failure.

Crates. The old Royal Flying Corps name for their aircraft and one which survives with the more recent KITES.

Creased. Tired out or fed up. A state bordering on the 'browned off' series.

Credits. Strange unexplained amounts sometimes added to a man's pay. All inquiries at Pay Accounts elicit the one mysterious word . . . 'Credits'.

Crib. To crib at something is to take exception to it and to say

25

as much; that something constitutes a crib, and people have their own pet cribs.

Crickets. German night-fighters.

Crook. Sick. [This rather suggests lead-swinging, or possibly 'crocked'].

Crown. The Major's, or the Sergeant-Major's, badge of rank. The one 'gets his Crown' as he gets his Majority, the other 'puts his Crown up' when he is made Company or Battery Sergeant-Major.

Crowns. The brass adornments worn above the three stripes and denoting a Sergeant's promotion to the rank of Flight-Sergeant.

Crumph. The noise made by the bursting of a shell or bomb.

The Crump dump. The Ruhr.

Crusher. Regulating Petty Officer, the Naval equivalent of a Military Policeman or Service Policeman.

Cu. Cumulus clouds.

The Curly Navy. The Royal Canadian Naval Reserve. [Variant of WAVY NAVY.]

Cuthbert. Another name for a conscientious objector.

Cutting the job up. Working too hard or getting the job done in less than the usual time. Or, by interpretation, attempting to curry favour with the N.C.O. in charge. See also MAKING IT BAD FOR OTHER PEOPLE.

Dados. The recently eliminated function of Deputy Assistant Director of Ordnance Services. (It is simply not true to say that δάδος is a Greek word meaning 'not obtainable'.)

Daisy roots. Slang for 'boots' which has survived from the Great War.

A Dart. A very quick try or last-minute effort.

Davy Jones's shocker. Torpedo.

Dawn hopper. A Hun plane whose pilot uses the uncertain light of daybreak to make for home.

Dead man's effects. The service name for false teeth.

Deck. The ground or landing-field. Men who were in the Naval Air Service in the last war say that this word was used in its correct place, referring as it did to aircraft landing on the deck of the ship from which they operated.

Dekko. A look. ('Let's have a dekko.') [From the Hindustani.]

Demmicks. Soldiers on the sick list, or articles of equipment unfit for service. Also DEMMICKED. [The word is at least as old as the Boer War and the derivation is probably 'epidemic-ked'.]

Depth charges. Prunes.

Dhobey day. Wash day. [Seaman's slang, from the Hindustani.]

Dinger. Yet another word for a telephone or bell system. In some camps it is used as a code message when one's girl friend rings up.

Dipped. Reduced to the ranks from N.C.O. status; deprived of one's prestige.

Dirt. Ack-ack fire.

Dirt on tapes. Signifies a certain length of service as an N.C.O. A newly made Corporal is always told by his senior N.C.O.s to get 'dirt' on his stripes because of their obvious newness on the background of a tunic which has seen some wear.

The Ditch. The sea.

Dock. The hospital or sick quarters.

Dodging the column. Shirking one's responsibilities or slacking at work. Taken from the old marching days when those at the back would slacken off because they were out of the Officer's sight. Applies equally to men who miss parades.

Dog. Yet another name for the sausage. The name should not be taken too seriously.

Dog clutch. Flying term for a disconnectable coupling.

Dog-fight. Aerial combat in which several machines are so mixed up in the fight that one cannot be distinguished from the other, as when dogs have a set-to and a mêlée ensues.

Dog-leg. A Good Conduct stripe is so called because it is shaped like a pair of legs, being the normal stripe in reverse.

Donkey's breakfast. The palliasse on which many men sleep; filled with straw, hence the title.

Don R. A motor-cyclist Dispatch Rider. ['Don' = 'D' in the old phonetic alphabet.]

Doodlebug. Utility truck, or light motor-van, as used by the Army. [Cf. JEEP.]

Doolally. Very drunk or temporarily insane, without distinction.

Dope. A mentally inert person.

Dorchester. See GIN PALACE [sense (*a*)].

Dos. Director of Ordnance Services—fountainhead of clothing and equipment.

Doughboy. American soldier.

A Drag. A draw at a cigarette, when that is all there's time for. Desperate characters when penniless will borrow lighted cigarettes or amalgamate discarded ends for 'just a drag'.

Dragon's teeth. A form of anti-tank obstacle.

Draped. The worse for drink—hanging on to lamp-posts or one's friend, i.e. draped round anything available.

Drawing a pint. Using the joystick or controls, an action similar to that employed behind public-house bars.

The Drill. The correct way of doing a job is always referred to in this manner, or as the 'right drill'.

The Drink. The English Channel. Coming down in the drink is, of course, the act of baling out over the Channel. [See other pages for nicknames for the Atlantic and the North Sea.]

Dripper. Naval term for one who is given to binding, a bore.

Dromestoners. The men who clear the aerodromes before runways are laid down.

Dropping a goolie. Making a serious blunder.

Drum up. To make tea [Army].

Drydock. This usually refers to an extended stay in hospital. (See DOCK.]

Drynumber. A man who has served several weeks is acknowledged to have 'dried his number'. [See HANG YOUR NUMBER OUT TO DRY.]

Dud weather. Unfit for flying.

Duff. (*a*) Pudding.

(*b*) Unreliable or useless. The adjective is connected in a serviceman's mind with GEN, as it almost invariably refers to news of an unconfirmed character or from an unreliable source.

Dustbin. The rear-gunner's position on a bomber, so called because of the shape of his little turret; also, a gun position on the under-side of the fuselage.

Duster. Naval slang for a flag.

Dust parade. Morning fatigue party for cleaning up.

Duty Dog. Orderly Officer or Duty Officer. A clerk on night duty, on the 'dogwatch'.

Ear-flip. A very cursory salute.

Ear-wigger. One who eavesdrops or butts in on other people's conversations.

Ear-wiggers. Headphones.

Eating irons. Knife, fork, and spoon.

Eggs. Bombs; a NEST is a stick of bombs.

Egg-whisk. The very apt nickname of the autogyro.

Ear-wigger

Elbow grease. The ancient term for hard work, such as removing rust from a steel surface when paraffin will *not* be used. Putting 'bags of elbow grease' into things means getting on with the job.

Elephant houses. Old forts at Dunkirk.

Elephant hut. A Nissen hut [shaped somewhat like the beast].

Elsan gen. News which cannot be relied upon. [Literally, 'news invented in the gentlemen's toilet', Elsan being the trade name of the excellent chemical lavatories with which bombers are equipped.]

Ensa. Abbreviated form of the well-known organization that is responsible for providing entertainments for the troops. E.N.S.A. is associated with N.A.A.F.I.

Erk. A common form of reference to recruits in the R.A.F. Originally, a lower-deck rating.

Everything under Control

Everything under control. All arrangements made and the job going ahead smoothly.

Eye lotion. Wines [only enough of them to provide an eye bath].

Fair do's. A fair arrangement.

Fair enough. The significance of this phrase is imprecise, and yet somehow very real. It may mean literally what it says, referring to a bargain, but it may also mean, for a subtle reason, 'This statement is plausible, you will agree [or, plausible, I agree].' The reason or the assumption is that if you wish to teach a soldier anything out of a book, you must appeal to his sense of fair play, not only to induce him to take a sporting interest in the subject, but also to convince him that he is not being fooled. The necessity to come to terms makes this a very useful phrase for anyone who has to give lectures.

Fan. Just another name for the propeller.

Fanad. Short for 'Sweet Fanny Adams', meaning none or nothing; no money, no knowledge of the matter, not a stroke of work, and so forth.

Fang farrier. Dentist.

A Fast one. (*a*) Any remark giving rise to Thought.

(*b*) A trick, especially one calculated to shift the onus. 'Pulling a fast one' on your associates is very much the same as 'putting one over' on them.

Father's backbone. This takes us back to an earlier state than that explored by even the most fanciful of contemporary psychoanalysts. '[I was playing snooker] when you were running up and down your father's backbone' is an old trooper's way of saying 'before you were born'.

Favourite. Odd-sounding at first, the word is most expressive as an adjective without a noun or a noun without an article. 'This is favourite'—this is best by popular vote or mutual consent.

Fiddle. To purloin or obtain by a wangle. Thus FIDDLER, one who is expert in fiddling.

Fighting cats. The Coat of Arms worn on the sleeves of Warrant Officers, Class One. Also known as GALLOPING HORSES in the R.A.F.

Find. To 'pick up' something which is needed by your section. Finding is generally less selfish than fiddling, and more silent than scrounging.

Firewatcher. One who can always be found by the fireside when his duties call for a little exposure. [An old meaning, which has no connection with A.R.P.]

Fireworks. Bomber crews give this name to intensive anti-aircraft fire. It is also used for flare dropping.

Fizzer. The Guardroom or room for detaining persons on charge or confined to camp.

Flag flapper. One of the Navy's names for a signaller.

Flak. Anti-aircraft fire. [From the German.]

Flaming onions. Tracer fire from the ground.

Flannel. Honeyed words or small gifts made to N.C.O.s with intent to ask favours.

Flap. State of panic or excitement. 'Enemy aircraft expected' constitutes a FLAP-ON at an aerodrome.

Flapping. A person who can't 'cope' or who is very nervous is told to stop 'flapping'.

Flare-up. Having a flare-up means losing one's temper, or alternatively, having a night out and lighting up the town.

Flat spin. When one is very busy and does not know which way to turn, one is 'in a flat spin' like an aircraft out of control.

Flimsies. The rice paper on which important messages are written and which can be eaten without discomfort in case of capture.

Flip. A trip in an aeroplane or in a car.

Floating one. Passing a dud cheque; organizing a loan with no definite security.

Flog. (*a*) To borrow without permission.

(*b*) To offer for sale (especially when financially embarrassed and attempting to raise funds for a binge).

The Flying cigar. The Wellington bomber (side view).

The Flying pencil. The Dornier bomber (side view).

The Flying suitcase. The Hampden and Hereford bombers (side view, forward section).

The Flying tin-opener. A name for the Hurricane tank-buster, or HURRI-BUSTER.

Fold up. To crash or go sick without warning.

Football feet. The disability of the pilot who uses too much rudder.

Fore and aft. Descriptive of a sailor's clothes, cut on the generous lines known to all.

Free and blowing. Same as above.

Foreigners. Although this word in the present sense is principally applied to workers outside the services, it has now taken root in some camps where men are able to make such things as models of aircraft, which they sell to friends. Such articles, made in the 'firm's' time and with the 'Company's' material, are called 'foreigners', as they are outside the normal work done by the employee or airman or soldier.

Fox. To mislead, to puzzle, to put off the scent, often by some cunning excuse or by a flow of technical jargon. A class may be foxed by the lecturer, an N.C.O. may be foxed by an OLD SOLDIER, an officer may be foxed by some unexpected turn of events.

Fred Karno's army. The army on Home Service, and particularly the specialist branches, regarded with a satirical eye.

Freeze. To send to Coventry.

Fruit machine. An anti-aircraft predictor.

Fruit salad. A large collection of medal ribbons which runs to three or more rows.

Gander. A look through the mail, a glance over another's shoulder at a letter or paper. To perpetrate this long-necked nuisance.

Gannet. Naval slang for a big eater, one whose appetite rivals that of the bird.

Gas face. Respirator anti-gas, or GAS-BAG.

The Gash. Waste food, anything surplus, an over-issue.

Gate. Flying term for full speed. THROUGH THE GATE—with open throttle.

Gen. A very common word meaning 'information'. Gen is subdivided into DUFF GEN or unreliable information, and PUKKA GEN which usually comes from an unimpeachable source or can be confirmed on the spot by undeniable proofs.

Gen king. The man who is 'in the know' and who can be relied upon to give advance news of promotions or postings, the chief topics of interest to serving men.

Geordie. A Newcastle man.

George. The name given to the automatic pilot. By switching over the controls, the pilot is able to rest and leave the command of the aircraft to 'George'. The saying 'Let George do it' may well have suggested this name.

Get a draft chit. Typically curt way of saying 'You're posted,' i.e. transferred to another unit.

Get a number. Rudely shouted to newly joined men, this infers they have not yet been allotted a number and that they have had a minimum of service. Even amongst N.C.O.s of considerable service the expression is still used to emphasize seniority by comparing numbers. The smaller the number, the greater the seniority in service—although this does not necessarily mean that the smallest number belongs to the man with the most stripes. It can be understood therefore that the inference is, at times, that the man with the small number should have the stripes worn by another.

Get cleaned up. Get ready to go on parade or to go out.

Get cracking. Get a move on; carry out your orders immediately.

Get knotted. A rude expression which is equivalent to putting one's tongue out.

Get mobile. Hurry up with the work, or get on parade; or, quite simply, commence. Get moving [i.e. play a Mobile not a Static role].

Get off your knees. An old favourite and one which suggests that the job is getting you down. It has nothing to do with scrubbing floors.

Get organized. (*a*) An American Sergeant's way of ordering 'Fall in' to a squad of men. [This definition is unconfirmed.] (*b*) To arrange one's kit or the work to be done in order before starting the day.

Get skates on. Get a move on: the job is urgent.

Get some service in. This is closely related to GET A NUMBER and carries the same implications.

Get stuck into it. Get down to the job; get on with it.

Getting a bottle. Being told off or dressed down by one's superior officer.

Getting his blood back. Revenging a friend's death by shooting down the enemy aircraft responsible.

Getting weighed off. Receiving punishment. [A Naval term.]

Get weaving. To GET CRACKING. This is a flying term and refers to the planes which circle round a formation to protect the rear from surprise attacks.

Get your head down. To lie down and go to sleep. (An oddly expressive phrase towards the end of a long spell.)

Get your knees brown. Men with Overseas Service to their credit tell Home Service chaps to do this.

Ghost. A Radio Officer.

Gibby. Naval word for a cap.

Gin palace. (*a*) Armoured Command Vehicle or 'Dorchester', constituting the headquarters of a brigade of an armoured division. The nerve centre of the armoured brigades.

(*b*) Any impressive interior, such as that of a static A.A. Command Post.

Gippo. Melted bacon fat.

Giz. To read a pal's letter to his girl friend—to offer advice.

Glasshouse. The old Army name for the Military Prison at Aldershot. It is now applied to any place of detention for long periods, and most big camps have some little room which is regarded locally as their 'Glasshouse'.

Gob. Nickname for an American sailor.

Goggled goblins. The pilots of our night-fighter squadrons.

Going ashore. A Wren's way of saying that she has finished her duties for the day; equivalent to 'Good night'.

Going to the movies. American pilots use this expression when they are going into action.

Golden Eagle. The Paymaster. In many camps, particularly in Southern England, they say 'Golden Eagle sits on Friday', which is self-explanatory.

Gone for a Burton

Gone for a Burton. Said of anyone who is missing as a result of a bomber trip or a fighter combat and of whom no news is received in a month. Cockney slang would be translated as 'Gone for Certain', though this might not be the truth.

Gong. A decoration worn on a full-dress parade. Doubtless the name is due to the noise made when medals 'jingle' on a well-covered chest.

Goon. The West Country name for recruit; apparently given because new arrivals are prone to walk about with a dazed expression until they have accustomed themselves to their surroundings.

Go take a running jump at yourself. Go to hell; buzz off.

Graft. Food and lodging. Thus GOOD GRAFT—comfortable living.

Grand Walloper. King of all the GREMLINS—their director of operations.

Gravel Bashing or **Square Bashing.** Marching drill on the parade ground, especially the intensive squad drill of the recruits' training period.

The Gravy. A pilot's name for the Atlantic. [See also THE POND.]

Grease. (*a*) Butter or margarine.

Gravel Bashers

(*b*) Small bribes or soft soap for getting time off [see also BUTTER]. One who wangles for time off is naturally called a GREASER.

Greenhouse. [See CONSERVATORY.] This is another name for the cabin of a bomber or troop-carrying plane.

Gremlins. The pixies which are supposed to haunt aircraft and persuade the pilots (especially learners) to do strange things. They sit on the wings and make faces at the air crew, thus taking their minds off the job in hand.

Griff. News [in Naval language; corresponding to GEN of the R.A.F.].

37

Grit. Food. (A gunner's word, heard in the Guardroom on a cold night.)

Grounded. A man who is medically unfit for flying duties is temporarily grounded for an examination by doctors, eye specialists, and so on. A man newly wed is often said to be in this position since he has to curtail many of his bachelor trips.

Ground-strafing. Low-flying attack on transport or trenches; careless driving by servicemen.

Groupie. Nickname for Group Captain in the R.A.F.

Gun. On 'getting his Gun', i.e. on being promoted from Lance-Sergeant to full Sergeant, an artilleryman wears a gun above his three stripes.

Gun buster. An artificer of the Royal Army Ordnance Corps; a TIFFY.

Gunfire. Early morning tea. So called because it often has to be of considerable strength to counteract a bad head.

Guns. The Gunnery Officer on a ship.

Gussies. Army nickname for the Officers.

Handing out slack. Using cheek to a superior officer or being rude to a colleague.

Hang your number out to dry. Another version of the GET A NUMBER series, and one which has been taken very seriously by many recruits. Some have been seen to hold their attestation forms out of carriage windows, in an endeavour to get the ink dry before reaching their depots.

Happy Valley. The area which is being heavily bombed, e.g. Cologne on the 1,000-bomber night.

Hard tack. Ship's biscuits.

Having kittens. Perturbed. 'The Colonel is having kittens'— the Colonel is upset and he is very, very angry.

An H.E. A severe reprimand.

A Heap. The same as A SHOWER [q.v.] in Army language, and even worse.

Heavies. Heavy guns. In ack-ack, for instance, the dividing line between heavy and light is the old 3-inch gun.

He bought it. He was shot down. HE BOUGHT A PACKET is another version.

Hedge-hopping. Flying low over hedges when being chased by the enemy, or when on a bombing raid, to avoid detection, to achieve surprise, to reduce the possible time of engagement by ground defences to a minimum, and to make interception by fighters extremely difficult.

Heel. This is an Americanism for a hanger-on, and in the service it means a fellow who seeks your company for the sake of a free drink. Thus HEELING, paying a heel for something.

Hit that silk. To bale out in a hurry. [American Air Force.]

Hogged. Tied down and unable to get off duty. [American Air Force.]

Hoggers. Day-dreaming. [Perhaps not unconnected with the after-effects of Hogmanay?]

Hoick off. To get airborne; to be on your way to somewhere.

Hold your horses. Hold the job up until further orders. [Comes from the Artillery.]

Hooching in quarters. Holding a party in one's room.

Hooky. Leading Seaman.

Hooshing. Purely an R.A.F. word, which means landing at great speed.

Hoovering. It is not difficult to understand that this word is connected with the now famous 'sweeps' by Fighter Command over Northern France. They get into all the corners!

Hopping the hound. Catching a train. [U.S.A. service slang.]

Hopping the twig. Having a fatal crash or meeting sudden death. [Canadian.]

Horizontal. The worse for drink.

Horrible man. Sergeant's sarcastic mode of address.

Horsing around. Playing practical jokes. [Canadian.]

Hot. Extremely proficient in one's job.

Huffy. A Waaf or A.T.S. who refuses one's invitation. [See also TOFFEE NOSE.]

Hulk. A damaged machine.

A Humdinger. Any fast aircraft or vehicle; any engine which runs really well.

Hurryback. Very appropriate name given to the Hurricane type of aircraft. And HURRI-BUSTER, the Hurricane tank-buster fitted with special heavy calibre guns.

I **mshi.** Clear off; GET CRACKING. [Army slang, from the Hindustani.]

Incident. There are no occasions, occurrences, or events in an airman's life. Anything that happens to him is an 'incident', and it is invariably recalled as such: why, nobody knows.

Insy. Short for incendiary bomb.

In the bag. To have the situation well in hand, or to know definitely that such and such a thing will happen, is to have it 'in the bag'. [Compare BUTTONED UP and WRAPPED UP.]

In the rattle. A Naval term meaning in detention, under arrest, or on a charge.

Ipe. Naval slang for a rifle.

Irish mail. Seaman's slang for potatoes.

Iron lung. Barrage Balloon boys' phrase for Nissen hut.

Irons. See EATING IRONS.

J **ab, A.** One of the numerous words for an inoculation.

Jacksie. Service slang for 'rear', 'tail', or 'bottom'.

Jankers. A mild form of detention, e.g. 7 days confined to camp. (A very popular word amongst the troops.)

Jarred off. Fed up or CHEESED OFF.

Jaunty. A Master at Arms.

Jeep. Another version of girl friend. There are also other definitions!

Jeep. The American and Canadian counterpart to our DOODLEBUG, used by the British for mobile warfare.

Jeep. A member of the Royal Canadian Naval Volunteer Reserve, the Canadian 'Wavy Navy'.

Jenny Wren. The popular nickname for a Wren. JILLTAR seems equally appropriate.

Jim Crow. Normally used to describe the corps of roof-spotters guarding our large buildings. Now taken into service slang to denote the man on watch when 'unofficial business', such as cards, is being transacted.

Jimmy-bungs. Seaman's slang for a cooper.

Jimmy the one. A First Lieutenant or 'Number One' of any ship.

Jinks. Quick turns in the air, a form of aerobatics and of avoiding action. JINKING, the act of carrying out sudden turning and diving.

The Joe Hunt. The man who gets all the dirty work to do.

Joe Soap. The 'dumb' or not so intelligent members of the forces. The men who are 'over-willing' and therefore the usual 'stooges'.

Join or **Join up.** Another polite way of telling someone to get a little service in, by suggesting that their offer of service has not yet been accepted by the forces.

Jonty. Naval nickname for the Master at Arms.

Joss. Luck. [An overseas slang word derived from the joss-stick.]

Jug. Army for detention or prison. 'Stir' is also used.

Juice. The North Sea. [See other pages for pilot's slang for the Channel and Atlantic.]

Jump on binders. To apply the brakes. [American-Canadian.]

Jump out of the window. Another form of 'baling out' and one really only applicable to planes with cabins—bombers, recce's, or troop carriers.

Jump sack. American name for the parachute.

Just the job. If you see anything that you like, whether it is something in a shop window or a new billet, this is what you say, meaning of course that it suits you all right.

'K' **Block.** Naval term for the 'Nuthouse' or place for the temporarily insane.

Kie. Seaman's slang for cocoa.

Killick. The Anchor worn by Petty Officers.

Kip. The good old Cockney Army name for bed and also for sleep. Thus, HAVE A KIP DOWN.

Kipper-kites. Aircraft engaged on convoy escort duties over the North Sea and usually giving protection to the fishing-vessels.

Kissing your aircraft good-bye. The act of baling out. One finds it hard to believe that pilots go to this trouble, attached though they may have been to their a/c.

Kites. A useful alternative to CRATES for describing aircraft. More appropriate in the last war when planes were only one stage beyond kites.

Kittens in a basket.

This new and expressive phrase is one of the few so far produced by members of the Women's Auxiliary Air Force and means that 'So and so' is friendly with 'So and so'.

Kittens in a Basket

42

Kiwi. A word brought over by the New Zealand airmen with a new meaning: men who do not belong to air crews. [The kiwi is a bird that does not fly.]

Knock off. (*a*) To purloin.

        (*b*) To finish work or whatever one is doing.

Lay On

Lay eggs. To lay mines, *not* to drop bombs.

Lay on. To arrange or organize.

Laid on. Confirming that transport and supplies are available, that men are on the spot, and, in short, that everything is ready for action.

Lancejack. Army for Lance-Corporal or Lance-Bombardier (one-stripe man).

Lash up and stow. To take down your hammock after a night's sleep and put it away.

43

Left right centre. To put your hat on straight; to drop your bombs on the target; in fact, to get everything just right.

Liaise. To get in touch or confer (with).

Liberty boat. The boat which takes men going on leave ashore.

Liberty buses. Free transport to take servicemen into the nearest town from isolated camps.

Limey. A British seaman. [Canadian slang. The Royal Navy introduced lime juice as a preventive against scurvy.]

Lineshoot. A tall story. [See SHOOTING THE LINE.]

Little Arthur. The Warden's pet name, now used by the R.A.F., for arsine gas.

Little Catherine. A field-gun of which the Russians are said to be very proud.

Lizzie. Nickname for the Lysander aircraft, so called because they are slow in comparison with modern planes of the Spitfire type. The machine is used for many tasks including Army Co-operation, rescue of pilots from the sea, and dropping of food, and it can still be used as a bomber. It has fixed under-carriage and the appearance, when in the air, of a huge prehistoric bird. Possibly the easiest type to identify.

Loaf. Cockney-*cum*-service name for one's head. USE YOUR LOAF is the injunction often heard when someone is particularly slow in following orders. But this phrase, in its finer meanings, says: 'Use your common sense. Interpret orders according to the situation as you find it, and don't follow the book of words too literally.'

Loot. Scottish slang for money received on pay day.

Loppy. Infected or lousy.

Lulu. What 'Mademoiselle from Armentieres' was to the soldiers of 1914–18, Lulu is to the modern airman. There is a popular song dedicated to this lady but the words at present used are, we regret, unsuitable for publication in this collection.

Made up. Promoted. (Applies to the stages from Corporal to Warrant Officer. From A.C. to L.A.C. one is 're-classified', and the first of the promotions is from L.A.C.—Leading Aircraftman and *not* Air Commodore as some airmen inform their friends—to the rank of Corporal.) MAKE UP, to promote.

Mae West. Slang for the life-jacket worn by pilots and other members of air crews.

Maggie. The Miles Magister trainer aircraft.

Make and mend. Off-duty hours. [Seamen used to be allotted certain times for making and repairing their clothes, and this practice has recently been reintroduced in A.A. Command.]

Makee-learn. Seaman's slang for a beginner.

Make one's number. To make oneself known in the right quarter [as a ship does on entering harbour].

Makes you think. A comment which often appears intensely humorous but which has no significance that we can define.

Making it bad for other people. Setting too good an example—on fatigues, for instance.

Malleted. Told off by an Officer. A new word to many of us but common in Gibraltar from whence it came.

Marmalade. The gold braid worn on the hats of Group Captains and above.

Matelot. A sailor, not necessarily of the Free French.

Matilda. An 'I' tank, heavily armoured and used for co-operation with Infantry; it was followed by the VALENTINE. Of late more has been heard of our Medium cruiser tanks, officially named like battleships the CRUSADER, the COVENANTER, the CHURCHILL.

Meanie. Someone who doesn't like paying his share.

Met. Eighth Army's word for enemy vehicles as opposed to tanks or guns. [From 'M.T.' for 'mechanized transport'?]

Met or Mets. The Meteorological Officer. [R.A.F.]

MICK

Mick. A seaman's hammock.

Mickey Mouse. The bomb-dropping mechanism on some types of bomber aircraft is so called because it strongly resembles the intricate machinery portrayed in Walt Disney's cartoons.

Midwaaf. An N.C.O. of the W.A.A.F. who is very officious with her girls.

The Milk Train. Appropriate name for the modern 'Dawn Patrol' on early morning reconnaissance flights.

Minions of the moon. Our night fighters and bombers.

A moan-on. One who is nursing a grouse or who is continually SHOOTING THE LINE about his or her misfortunes.

Moldy. A torpedo. [Canadian slang.]

Molotov bread-basket. A bunch of incendiaries which blow out in a group as they drop to the ground.

Molotov cocktail. An anti-tank fire ball in the form of a bottle containing a combustible mixture and fitted with a fuse.

Moppie. Member of a cleaning party.

More than that. A Naval expression emphasizing that their party, job, or pay exceeds anything you can put forward in competition.

The Mount. One's bicycle.

Muck. Dirty weather.

Muck in. To join in with your companions, especially when roughing it; to do your share and be a mate.

Mucking-in spud. One's chum, i.e. the man who shares your company and your thoughts. 'Spud' is used in some camps to denote 'pal'.

Mucking. The Indian Army slang for butter and used by those who have served in that country.

Mudhook. Army name for the Crown and Anchor board used surreptitiously by members of the forces.

Muscle in. An Americanism for 'join in' or 'get in on' but suggesting that the person does this without an invitation, i.e. elbows his way through a crowd using his arm muscles.

Mush. The GLASSHOUSE or guardroom.

Naffy. The services are supplied on land and sea by the N.A.A.F.I. (Navy, Army, and Air Force Institutes). There are fully equipped shops and grocery stores in addition to the station canteens and mobile canteens which serve outposts.

Naffytime. The morning break.

Natter. To chide or chatter in an irritatingly aimless fashion.

Natter party. A Conference which leads nowhere.

Navvy's wedding cake. Service slang for the time-honoured Bread Pudding.

Needled. Inoculated before overseas service.

Nelson's blood. The Naval rum issue.

Nibbling. Courting or taking out a girl fairly regularly.

No future in it. The air crew's comment on a particularly hazardous job of work which they have taken on.

Nose scratch. Self-explanatory as a type of salute usually given by rookies. 'Peek a Bo' is another description of that salute.

Not a sausage. No luck, nothing to come on pay day, not a plane in the sky; nothing at all. Evidently the humble sausage is the lowest of the low for it rests on the verge of non-existence.

Nursery. A training station, usually for flying 'personnel'. Thus, NURSERY SLOPES, the easy targets allotted to beginners on bombing tests.

Nursery Slope

Octu. Officer Cadet Training Unit. The training has become so hectic that PRE-OCTU courses are necessary.

The Office. Yet another name for the cockpit or cabin on an aircraft.

Ogo-pogoing. A new slang term claimed by the R.A.F. and which is interpreted as 'looking for unidentified aircraft'.

Oil. Army for tea, due to the fat which often appears on top.

Old buck. Cheek; answering back and being rude.

Old iron. There are two definitions which enjoy equal popularity. The first is claimed by bicycles and the second is attributed to any copper coins which an airman will risk in a card game or raffle.

The Old man. The Skipper of any ship.

Old Newton. Gravity, the pilot's foe. ('Old Newton stretched out his hand and took him.')

Old rope. Any tobacco which offends the nostrils of those

Old Rope

present, and especially the finer varieties such as Egyptian.

Old soldier. (*a*) A veteran in terms of service and experience, not necessarily of age.

(*b*) One who, by reason of his long service and experience, or by a premature intuition, is able to escape some of his liabilities as a private soldier, or who is adept at TELLING THE TALE. (Old soldiers, in the good as well as the derogatory sense, seldom seek promotion, although they usually wear Good Conduct stripes on the lower portion of the sleeve.)

Old sweat. Universal favourite for an OLD SOLDIER [sense(*a*)]

On stag. On sentry duty as a roving picket; on the prowl.

On tap. Available at a moment's notice. [From Civvy Street, of course.]

On the beach. Retired from the sea.

On the beam. I follow what you are saying. [R.A.F.]

On the mat. Used in the services as in Civvy Street to mean: having a telling-off from one's superior officer.

On the Pegs

On the peg or **pegs.** On a charge.

Oojah. Sauce or custard.

Oolala. Army French meaning O.K. or 'hot stuff'.

O Pip. An Observation Post of the Field Artillery. ['Pip' stood for 'P' in the services' phonetic alphabet.]

Opposite number. The person whose function corresponds to your own and with whom you LIAISE and co-operate [listed opposite your name in the other watch in the muster book].

D   49

My Oppo. Chum. [Used by the Marines where the Navy would say MY CHINA.] 'Oppo' is sometimes used in the Navy to mean 'sweetheart'.

Orderly dog. Orderly Officer.

Organize. To organize a squad is to put them through their initial training and so make a *squad* out of *individuals*.

An Outside view. View from the air of the target.

Packet, A. It contains Trouble.

Pack it up or **in.** Stop talking or fooling; cut it out.

Pack up. Cease work.

Paint a picture. To describe a situation, or to indicate in general terms what is to be done. (A conveniently vague phrase, very popular in the early days of the war.)

Pan. Slang for face. Also used instead of 'hit', i.e. to 'pan' a man is to strike him.

Pan. Naval slang for bread. [Canadian, from the French.]

Pancake. To land. The order given in the air is 'Pancake' and this is part of the standard air language.

Panic. To lose one's head or to get very hot and bothered about a job. (This word is connected with moments of great activity such as the visit of a very high official.)

Panic party. The Naval version of a FLAP-ON.

Parting brass-rags. A very good Naval expression for quarrelling between close friends. [They share cleaning materials, and to fall out therefore means dividing the rags so that each cleans in his own quarters.]

A Party. A bombing raid or a combat would normally be a party in the language of a pilot. A very busy day would also be described in this manner by other service men.

Pash. To the Navy this means a letter; NUMBER ONE PASH being a letter to one's best girl.

Pay-bob. Naval slang for the Paymaster.

The P.B.I. Universal designation of the 'poor bloody Infantry'.

Peace-time soldier. One whose Army job is the same as his civil job, e.g. a Unit draughtsman.

Like a Pea in a colander. Running round in small circles; agitated; jumpy.

Peashooters. The guns or cannon on our aircraft.

Peel off. A form of aerobatics used in combats: to break away from a formation in order to meet an attack, or to leave a squadron to initiate an attack.

Peeping Tom. A pilot who is an expert bad weather flyer and can dodge from cloud to cloud.

Pegged. Placed on a charge.

Pegging a date. Making an appointment. [U.S.A.]

Penguin. An Officer on the Ground Staff of the R.A.F.

Penny packets. Small parties of soldiers, less than a platoon, as seen from the air.

Perpetrate a nonsense. To issue an order. [Local A.A. slang.]

A Piece of cake. A cakewalk or a snip; a thing that is easy to handle or an unmistakable opportunity, e.g. a clear prospect of promotion.

Pigs are up. The barrage balloons are up.

Pig-sticker. Bayonet. [This is an overseas version.]

Pile up. To crash in a plane.

Pimple. The cover of a gun position which is just visible above the fuselage of a plane.

Pip. The lowest common factor of commissioned badges of rank in the Army. Smith 'has got his pip'—has been granted a commission.

Pip-squeak. The pilot's term for his radio telephony set.

Pip, Squeak, and Wilfred. The three medals awarded for Mons, General Service, and Victory.

Piston. The nickname for any Engineering Officer.

Pitch a woo. To start a courtship.

Plates of meat. Rhyming slang for feet.

51

Play. (*a*) To reciprocate, as between one H.Q. or department and another. A proposal is put forward, and the higher formation may or may not 'play'.

(*b*) N.C.O.s who believed in Compromise as a method of rule have sometimes been heard to say, 'If you play (play fair, play the game, play ball) with me, I'll play with you' [i.e. see that you get your time off].

Play pussy. To take advantage of cloud cover, jumping from cloud to cloud to shadow a potential victim or avoid recognition.

Pleep. The note of a high klaxon; a Hun pilot who turns tail.

A.C. Plonk. The lowest form of service life, to wit, Aircraftman, Second Class.

Plue. Seaman's slang for tea.

Plug away. To keep on trying; to stick to the enemy or to bang away at the target until it is destroyed.

Plumber. An armourer in the R.A.F.

The Pond. The Atlantic. Sometimes called THE HERRING POND.

Pongo. A soldier [in Naval slang].

Poodle faking. Getting dressed up for ashore or for the town; going after a SKIRT or girl.

Poop off. To fire (with heavy artillery).

A Poor view. If you do not agree with a statement or with your C.O.'s ruling on a certain matter or, in fact, with the world in general, you TAKE A POOR VIEW.

Popeye. The Observer on an aircraft; the Look-out on a ship.

Popsies. Girl friends. [See also BINT.]

Poultice plasterer. Naval slang for the Medical Officer, also called the QUACK.

Poultice walloper. Sick berth attendant.

Pozzie. Jam.

P.P. Abbreviated form of 'privilege pass', the card entitling one to be out of camp during the day. For overnight passes a special form, the TWO-NINE-FIVE, is used.

Prang. A crash. ['P/O Prune' is the title bestowed upon a pilot who has several 'prangs' on his record.] To crash or smash [sometimes applied to non-flying accidents, e.g. 'Jones pranged his arm at rugger to-day.']

Praying mantis. A tail landing, whether accidental or intentional if the undercarriage fails to work.

The Priest. A self-propelling field gun in use by the Eighth Army.

Props. The propeller-shaped badge worn on the sleeve by Leading Aircraftmen of the R.A.F. (This has no connection with flying duties and is awarded in all trades, being the stepping-stone between A.C., First Class and Corporal.)

Prune. A pilot who takes unreasonable risks, and generally loses his neck through his PRUNERY.

Pukka. Correct [especially of news or GEN which can be relied upon]. The PUKKA SAHIB is, of course, always pictured as the example of British local rule, the sportsman and the man who can be trusted.

A Pull. Influence or sway; generally, in effect, a friend in the right quarter.

Pulling a pint. Operating the controls or BEER LEVERS, i.e. doing the job of a pilot.

Pulling his Scotch. Leg-pulling. [Apparently a reference to the alleged lack of humour in Scotsmen.]

Pull-off. A parachute jump off the wing of a machine. In this case a man opens his parachute and is then pulled off. [Para-troops' slang.]

Pull your finger out. Wake up—get a move on.

Pulpit. Yet another version of 'cockpit'.

Pulverizer. Nickname for the giant Stirling bomber, and very apt too.

Punctured. Vaccinated.

Purge. A concentrated complaint or moan from a well-known source is called 'a purge-on by So and so'. An habitual grumbler is called by this name in many places.

A Pusher. Nickname for a girl friend.

Pusser. Naval. [From 'purser'.]

Put a squeak in. To make a complaint, whether verbally or by letter to a Senior N.C.O. or Officer.

Put you in the picture. To give you, as a new-comer, an idea of what is happening (by PAINTING THE PICTURE) and so enable you to play your part in it.

Q, The. The QUARTERBLOKE or Quartermaster-Sergeant.

Quad. A *four*-wheel drive tractor used for towing field-guns.

Queen At. A Chief Commander of the A.T.S.

Queen bee. A plane used for anti-aircraft firing practice, having no crew and controlled by radio from the ground. (Not a new invention.)

Quickie. A rapid burst of fire from machine-guns at close range.

Quick squirt. Machine-gun firing from fighter aircraft. Hundreds of bullets are fired in a few seconds from, say, each of eight guns.

Quisling. In the services, as outside, this denotes a traitor and, more often than not, a tell-tale. One who seeks favours sometimes acts as an N.C.O's. quisling.

Rattle, The. The [Naval] defaulters' report.

Rat-trap. Submarine.

Recce. Has for all practical purposes replaced the full words 'reconnaissance' and 'reconnoitre'; often used for 'reconnaissance plane'.

Red-cap. A Military Policeman.

The Red Shield. The clubs run by the Salvation Army in many camps and towns. 'Gone to the Red Shield' is the familiar answer to 'Where's George?'

Red tape. Requires no explanation. One new definition is, the red band worn by the Military Police.

Reemy. The Royal Electrical and Mechanical Engineers, formed in 1942 for the repair of Army tanks, transport, ordnance, and electrical equipment.

Rhino. This means money: why, it is difficult to imagine. Perhaps a reader will be able to throw light on the matter.

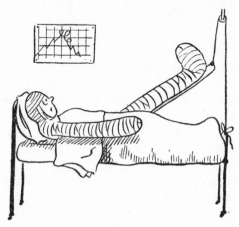

Bound Rigid

Rigid bind. A perpetual bore who bores you stiff!

Rings. Abbreviated reference to an Officer's rank, denoted in the Navy and R.A.F. by the number of rings on his sleeve.

Ring the bell. To hit the target; to hit the nail on the head; to win an argument by proving one's statement. [Taken from the fairground game of registering one's strength by sending a block of wood up to strike a bell at the top of a high contraption.]

Rock. To startle someone with your news. [A new version of SHAKE.]

A Rocket. A severe telling-off from an Officer, and generally to a junior Officer, and especially by the Brigade Commander or the C.O.; also administered by higher formations to lower formations. Another word for this is Raspberry.

Roller-skates. Tanks.

Roman candles. 'When a parachute simply fails to open. (Of course, on landing, you dash to the stores and get another.)' [From a Paratroop.]

Roof-spotters. The accepted name for those who watch for enemy aircraft on large buildings is now used in the Army and R.A.F., which have roof-spotters of their own.

Rookie. Recruit. Perhaps the best of all nicknames for a newly joined man or woman.

Rookettes. A charming word for female recruits.

Rooty gong. Long Service Medal. [Indian Army term.]

Ropey. Dilatory. Said of a person who is careless about his appearance or one who makes frequent mistakes.

Round shot. Peas again—this description comes from Gibraltar.

Rubber heels. Hard fried eggs.

Rum. A Naval word meaning 'bad'. [Cf. SCRAN.]

Rumble. To tumble to something or somebody, or catch him out.

Running rabbit. A small object hauled along a horizontal wire for predictor layers who are in the first stages of learning to follow a target.

Sack of taters. A stick of bombs.

Sad apple. A serious type of fellow who doesn't go to parties. [U.S.A.]

Salt beef squire. A Warrant boatswain.

Sardine tin. Bren Gun carrier.

Sawn off. Neat way of referring to a small Pilot; for example, 'Sawn Off' Lock, D.S.O., D.F.C., etc.

Scapathy. State of mind and feeling after being stationed for some time in the Orkneys. Another word for this form of being browned off is ORKNEYITIS.

Scarlet slugs. Apt name for Bofors tracer fire.

The Score. The number of drinks consumed or the bill to be paid.

Scotch mist. Sarcastic comment on your eyesight, inferring that you are seeing things.

Scramble. Aircraft taking off after the enemy. SCRAMBLE or SCRAM, to take off.

Scran. A Naval word meaning 'good'. [Cf. RUM.]

Screamer. A whistling bomb, i.e. a bomb with a device attached to cause a screaming sound as it descends.

Screaming Downhill

Screaming downhill. Making a power dive in a fighter aircraft. [A definite whistling noise is caused by the wind and, we believe, the airscrew on certain types.]

Scrub it. Cancel it, wash it out.

57

Scrub round. To wash off the slate, to agree to forget, to let bygones be bygones.

Scuttle. To disappear—the Nazis are exponents of the art but some A.C.s have been known to vanish pretty quickly when required by an N.C.O.

Segs on the dooks. A most descriptive term which, translated, means 'hard skin on the hands caused by heavy work'. Very popular amongst transport drivers.

Senior soldier. Not a slang term, but one which should be known and carefully distinguished from OLD SOLDIER where necessary. In any party where no Officer or N.C.O. is present, the Senior Soldier is the man with the greatest length of service. In the Guards Regiments, a Senior Soldier is placed in charge of each barrack room of recruits and the

This'll shake 'em

58

penalty for failing to address him as 'Senior Soldier', or showing disrespect to him, is likely to prove heavier than for a corresponding lapse with an N.C.O., so they say.

Seven-beller. Cup of tea.

Sewn up. See BUTTONED UP.

Shagbats. Coastal Command nickname for the Walrus aircraft.

Shake. To administer a shock. [See THAT SHOOK HIM.]

A Shaky do. An affair which has been mismanaged, a 'poor show'.

A Shocker or **Complete Shocker.** A hopeless individual or object—simply terrible.

Shooting the line. Bragging; telling a tall story; exaggerating.

Shot down. Pulled up for not saluting or for being improperly dressed; defeated in an argument by a decisive point.

Shot down in flames. Very severely told off, or proved wrong without a shadow of doubt.

Shot up. Hopelessly drunk. And SHOT TO RIBBONS—in the worst possible state from the same cause.

A good Show. A very successful combat, a highly satisfactory advance, a promotion, or, in fact, anything which calls for congratulation. Conversely, A BAD SHOW.

A Shower. [In the Army.] A detachment or individual whose ways are slack and whose turn-out is slovenly; hence SHOWERY. [In the R.A.F.] 'What a shower' is the derisive remark hurled at someone who has just made a blunder.

Silver sausage. The Barrage Balloon.

Sinkers. Doughnuts.

A Skinful. (a) Enough of being ticked off or listening to another's woes; a 'bellyful' of this.

(b) 'One over the eight.'

Skirt. A girl; or, girls collectively.

Skirt patrol. A walk in search of female company.

Skypiece. Smoke trails or sky-writing.

Sky pilot. Universal nickname for the Padre.

On the Slate. In many cafés a credit system is employed whereby amounts owing are entered on a slate which is wiped clean when payment is forthcoming.

Sleeve. A cylindrical pennant towed across the sky on the end of a very long tow line as a target for anti-aircraft firing practice.

Slingers. Sausage, according to Gibraltar.

Sling your hook. To clear off [take down your hammock before joining another ship].

Slops. Sailors' clothes. The SLOP CHEST is their Clothing Stores.

Slurge. A very ROPEY recruit—a disgrace to his service. The black sheep of the squad.

Slushy. Ship's cook.

A Small go. A reasonable night out with everybody happy and nobody drunk.

Smashing. A tremendously popular word, especially in the Army, meaning excellent or marvellous and applied to any object worthy of admiration. One feels that a 'smashing job' is related to a 'smash hit'.

Smig. A Sergeant-Major Instructor in Gunnery.

Smoothie. A chap who fancies himself as a ladies' man. [Often applied to a good dancer by non-dancing airmen.]

Snake about. To take evasive action when pursued by enemy fighters or when illuminated by searchlights and engaged by ack-ack.

Snargasher. A type of training aircraft. [This is Canadian slang and refers to smashing up the tarmac.]

Snobber. Naval nickname for cobbler, used also in the Army (e.g. 'Battery snob'). Even in civil life a snob is a shoemaker, and there is a strong case for assuming that shoemakers were the original snobs.

Snoop. To pry or ferret into business not your own. Sometimes rudely associated with the Service Police because their business is to question your movements should these be open to doubt.

Snotty. Midshipman. [So called after the buttons on his sleeve, which are said to be there for a purpose not unconnected with the nickname.]

Snow. Slang word for silver coins.

A Soft number. An easy job or 'cushy billet' as was said in the last war. Often associated with a clerical post or a job well away from the 'front'.

Sorted out. To pick a quarrel and use force is to 'sort out' someone. 'Who sorted me out for this one?' means: 'Who thought of giving me *this* job?'

Spanjers. GREMLINS which live above 20,000 feet—anti-fighter types!

Sparks. Nickname for the radio operator.

Spats. Streamline fairings which do not completely cover the undercarriage legs of a plane. If the wheels of a 'spatted' plane do not retract, it is said to have 'permanent spats'; for instance, in Lysanders and some training aircraft. [Cf. TROUSERS.]

Spit and polish. Without mention of the time-honoured recipe for self-smartening, this book would be more incomplete than it is.

Spitter. Apt nickname for that famous fighter the Spitfire, pride of the R.A.F. Also known as SPIT.

Sprog. (*a*) Chum or friend.
(*b*) Recruit or rookie.

Sprucing. Trimming the truth; or, pulling someone's leg.

Spud. Pal. [See also MUCKING-IN SPUD.]

Spud-basher. A man on cookhouse fatigue for potato peeling.

Spud hole. The Guardroom.

Spun in. A tactical error admitted. [To spin is dangerous.]

Squaddie. Recruit—new to the squad. [An American term.]

The Square. One's early days on drills are spent on the large parade ground called 'the Square'. Even during off-duty hours, complex laws come into play when one steps off the road on to the Square.

ON THE SQUARE

On the Square. Honest or on the level.

Square-pusher. A chap who is trying to get a girl. A chap who has a date.

Squeezebox. A concertina in the last war, and a piano-accordion in this.

Squirt. [See QUICK SQUIRT.] A burst of machine-gun fire.

A Stab. When one man has failed to do a job, another will exclaim 'Let's have a stab [or CRACK] at it.'

Staff. Staff Sergeant.

Stand-in. A deputy; one who 'stands in' for you, or does your duty while you go out.

Stand on everything. To put the brakes on or hold up a job for amended instructions.

Stand on one leg. To be caught doing something in official hours [i.e. to be in an awkward position].

Stationmaster. Station Commander. His conferences are always known as STATIONMASTER'S MEETINGS.

A Steady man. One who is so slow as to be practically useless.

Stick of bombs. A number of bombs, usually four, dropped together.

Sting. To inoculate with a hypodermic needle.

Stitched. The worse for drink.

Stokes. Anyone employed in the stoking side of the ship.

Stooge. The 'stand-in' or the deputy. Also, someone who always volunteers for extra work; an over-willing chap.

Stooging. On patrol. Monotonous flying over the same ground.

Stop one. To have the misfortune to be on the spot, or held responsible, when trouble comes [to get in the way of a fast ball or a bullet].

Stop a packet. To come in for severe trouble (probably through your own fault).

Store-basher. One who works in the Stores.

Straight up. Honest. And in your anxiety to show that a statement is authentic, you prefix it with 'Straight up, . . .'

On Strap. On credit.

Strawberry. A bouquet from the C.O., infinitely more rare than the RASPBERRY.

A Strike. A planned attack on enemy possessions.

Stringbag. The Swordfish torpedo-bomber ('Stringbag the Sailor').

Stripey. A long service A.B. One with many badges who is still an Ordinary Seaman.

Stripped. Reduced to the ranks from N.C.O. status; or, relieved of one stripe. It often happens that a man is in an 'Acting' rank and, at the termination of some particular duties, reverts to the rank formerly held.

Stuffy. Standoffish or snobbish; not easily making friends; unsociable.

Sub. A loan of money.

Sub-mariners. The crews of our submarines.

Sudden death. Quick ending to a game of darts or anything else.

Swamped. Having had one over the eight; DRAPED.

Swanks. Best clothes, i.e. BEST BLUE. Thus, SWANK, to dress in one's grandest attire; to prepare to meet a girl.

Sweating on. The symptoms of one who anticipates promotion or posting are called 'sweating on', which infers that he is getting hot and bothered about it.

Swede-basher. Agricultural worker; country bumpkin.

A Sweep. An offensive patrol over a wide area, carried out by a large formation of fighters or bombers or a combination of both; the formation itself.

Swinging the lead. An old Naval term derived from the duty of measuring the depth of water by casting a leaden weight or plumb line in the sea. Commonly understood to mean avoiding one's rightful tasks or slacking, i.e. swinging the lead instead of casting it.

Synthetic. Often applied to news which is suspect, or to a person who seems to pretend to be something more than he really is.

Tail-end Charlie. The Rear Gunner on a bomber.

Take a poor view. To disapprove. This humorously impersonal phrase is typical of a certain spirit and very popular. One takes a poor view of anything, from being badly let down by somebody to being detailed for some invidious task.

Take a dim view. To take an extremely poor view.

Taking a Poor View

Take a gloomy view. This, on the contrary, means to be depressed about something.

Take felt. It is fashionable to speak of 'taking felt' instead of being BOWLER-HATTED [q.v.], which is now considered a rather crude way of putting it.

Taking it on. [Of an aircraft.] Climbing very rapidly.

Tally ho. Flying term for 'Enemy sighted'.

Tangled in the soup. Lost in the fog. [R.A.F.]

Tank-buster. Aircraft fitted with heavy calibre guns for knocking out A.F.V.s.

Tapes. The stripes worn by Corporals, Sergeants, and Flight Sergeants in the R.A.F. and by Lance-Corporals or Lance-Bombardiers, Corporals or Bombardiers, and Sergeants in the Army. Not in general use in the Navy where 'stripes' is the word.

Taps. The controls and gadgets of a modern aircraft.

Tash. Moustache.

Tatered. Fed up with having no luck or with unproductive patrols.

Taxi-driver. An instructor at a wireless and navigation training school. [Cf. BUS DRIVER.]

Tear him off a strip. To tell him off severely. Officers and

N.C.O.s do this, and even his girl tears off a strip when he forgets a date with her.

Teased out. Worn out or tired after a long spell of flying or other duty.

Tee up. A golfing term now adopted in the R.A.F. to denote 'Time to get ready' for a flight or for a parade.

Tally ho

Telling the tale. Drawing the long bow; explaining things in the manner of an OLD SOLDIER.

The Terriers. The Territorial Army is embodied and no longer exists as a separate entity, but the old name survives.

E 65

TOOTS

Tewts or **Toots.** Technical Exercises Without Troops. ('You are in command of . . . You receive the following information . . . What are you going to do about it?')

That shook him—when someone advised him that he'd been posted or that his rival had been promoted to the position he himself coveted. A popular phrase which is more or less self-explanatory.

That's my story and I'm stuck all round it. A lengthy expression emanating from the Royal Engineers. It is used to confirm an alibi and to indicate that one is not likely to be moved from the version given.

That thing is wild. The aircraft is much faster than was thought.

Thick. The opposite of bright; the opposite of smart; the opposite of keen.

Three-pointer. A three-point landing, i.e. all wheels down. Used to describe a 'perfect' fall on the playing-field or elsewhere.

Throw one up. To salute in good style.

Ticket. One's discharge paper. Regarded (though this should not be taken too seriously) as the ambition of every soldier and airman. To go sick for a trivial illness is to start working on one's Ticket, and it would be difficult to go through a day in which this word did not crop up. For whether it rains or whether something goes wrong on the job, the conclusion of the temporarily or permanently depressed is always 'Wait until I get my Ticket!'

Tiddley. (*a*) Alcoholically happy.

(*b*) In Naval language, dressed up for a parade or a day ashore.

Tiddly Oggy. A Cornish pasty. [Naval term.]

Tied up. Everything organized. [See also BUTTONED UP, WRAPPED UP, SEWN UP, IN THE BAG, and EVERY-THING UNDER CONTROL.]

Tiffy. An artificer of the R.A.O.C. Also applied, though incorrectly, to gun fitters of the R.A.

Tiffy bloke. An engine-room artificer.

Tilly. Short for Utility truck. [See also UTE and DOODLE-BUG.]

Tin fish. Torpedo.

Tin hat. Steel helmet.

Tin titfor. Steel helmet. [Seagoing term.]

Tit. Gun button.

Toffee-nose. Another of the expressions chiefly heard amongst the W.A.A.F. This refers to a snob or someone who considers herself 'superior'. It is very apt since it implies that the nose is kept high to prevent it coming into contact with the mouth.

Tooling along. Walking aimlessly or flying with no fixed objective.

Tools. Knife, Fork, and Spoon.

A Toot. A complaint, or a MOAN-ON.

Topsides. Having the final say in any particular matter of military organization. [Pidgin English.]

Torps. A Torpedo Officer.

Touch-bottom. A crash landing.

Tour of miseries. The day's work when one is feeling down in the mouth.

Toys. The mechanical parts of a plane so beloved by the armourers and flight mechanics who care for the machines.

The Trade. The name given to the Submarine Service. If ever there was a man's trade, this deserves the name by which it is known.

Train driver. The leader of a large formation, i.e. a Wing or Sweep of several squadrons.

Treacle. To flatter someone, usually senior to oneself; to administer soothing syrup.

The Troops. The Ship's Company.

Trousers. The streamline covering in which the undercarriage legs of some planes are enclosed; such planes being TROUSERED. [Cf. SPATS.]

Tug. An aircraft which tows glider-borne troops.

Turn up the wick. Open the throttle.

Twirp. A rather rude word to describe someone whom you consider useless and of whom you have a very poor opinion.

Two and half bloke. A Lieutenant-Commander, having two thick rings and one thin one on his sleeve.

Two-Five-Two. The official number of the charge-sheet form, by which it is commonly known in the Army and R.A.F.

Two-Nine-Five. The number of the leave or pass form, so very much sought after by airmen and waafs.

Type. An Officer whether of the R.A.F. or another service. 'Brown type' (Army Officer) and so on.

Undercart. The undercarriage of an aircraft.

Up the creek. Lost, either on patrol or during a night out; off one's course.

Up the line. To a sailor, 'going up the line' means 'going on leave'.

Up the rock. Under detention in Gibraltar.

Up the spout. On loading a rifle or gun, i.e. inserting or ramming a round into the chamber, you have 'one up the spout'.

U.S. Unserviceable; damaged or broken.

Use your loaf. See under LOAF.

Ute. Short for Utility truck, a light van used by the Army.

Very grave. When finances are low you will often hear, in reply to a question, the words 'Very Grave', or 'THE POSITION IS CRITICAL.' This has nothing to do with defeatist talk but is merely a polite way of letting the world know that you are broke.

Waaf. Member of the Women's Auxiliary Air Force.

Waafery. The part of the camp frequented, or the billets occupied, by members of the W.A.A.F.

Wad. Service slang for cake.

Waffling. [Of an aircraft.] Out of proper control—spinning or losing height.

Waffle. To discourse without precise knowledge of one's subject. [This adaptation comes from OCTU, where Cadets lecture on what they have recently learnt.] To dither.

Wailing Winnie. Broadcast system aboard ships. *Not* the air raid sirens.

Wake your ideas up. Pull yourself together; abandon that lazy attitude of mind.

Wallah. A fellow of any kind, from a Camouflage wallah (Camouflage Officer) to a Sanitary wallah (Sanitary Orderly). Or collectively, e.g. the Ordnance wallahs. [The word is used rather more by Officers than by other ranks in the Army. Compare BLOKE, which is synonymous.]

Wallop. The favourite name for Beer where servicemen are concerned.

Watch your step. Be careful or take care. This is usually issued in the form of a threat after you have offended someone of the bully type.

Waves. Volunteer 'Wrens' of the U.S. Navy.

The Wavy Navy. The Royal Naval Volunteer Reserve. [An expression which dates from the beginning of the last war, and which very soon became an honoured name.]

Well bottled. Tight or drunk. [See DRAPED and SWAMPED.]

Wheels down. Prepare to land, i.e. get ready to leave the train or bus. [Taken from the lowering of the undercarriage which is necessary to enable a modern plane to make a good landing.]

Whirligig. The Whirlwind fighter.

A Whistler. A high explosive bomb descending. [See also SCREAMER.]

Whizzbang. A Fighter on the tail of an enemy aircraft.

Whizzucks. GREMLINS which live on the outskirts of enemy aerodromes.

69

Wimpey. The nickname for that famous heavy bomber the Wellington, one of the finest aircraft in the R.A.F. and the first to take part in bombing operations against Germany in the Kiel Canal raid of September 1939. Twin-engined with large single fin.

Win. To obtain something by dubious methods; to purloin.

Wind in your neck. A polite way of asking someone to close a door. Often used when people are in bed in a billet and someone comes in late and forgets to shut the door, thereby causing a draught which catches the necks of the sleeping personnel.

Windmill. Another nickname for the autogyro or EGG-WHISK.

Wise boys' paradise. This very apt term is used in the services to describe the *unimportant* jobs which seem to keep many eligible men out of uniform, and the places overseas to which men have gone to avoid conscription.

Wizard. An American word which had a vogue at Oxford and now enjoys tremendous popularity in the R.A.F. Meaning excellent or marvellous, this may describe a combat, a new aircraft, or perhaps a good-looking waaf. [We have a habit of dropping the article when we borrow from American slang. An American would never say 'It's wizard', as we often do. The original phrase was 'It's a wizard'.]

Wom. Abbreviated form of Wireless Operator (Mechanic), used freely in the R.A.F.

Wops. Nothing to do with Italy, but short for Wireless Operators.

Wrap up. Stop talking. Or, to get ready to go home.

Wrapped up. See BUTTONED UP, etc.

Wren. Member of the Women's Royal Naval Service.

Wrennery. Billets of the 'Jenny Wrens'.

A Write-off. Something beyond repair which must be written off the station inventory.

Yellow doughnut. The small collapsible dinghy carried on modern aircraft—it looks like a doughnut from the air.

You ring the bell. You are accepted; you are O.K. by the chaps.

You've been. A visit or trip in an aircraft which was promised has been cancelled.

You've had it. A characteristic way of saying that you've arrived too late for pay, letters, or parade. In short, you've missed the boat.

Yum yum. Love letters [the Navy again].

Zizz. A rest period. Slackers' paradise.